I0659114

Best of the
Robert Hines Collection

An incomplete collection of works by the Deep Ellum Poet

Best of the
Robert Hines Collection
ISBN 978-0-9976535-3-3
Copyright by Robert Hines and Cheudi Publishing
First Printing Summer 2020

All rights reserved. No part of this work may be reproduced or transmitted in any form or by any means, electronic or mechanical, including photocopying, recording or any information storage retrieval system, without the expressed written permission from the Publisher.

Cheudi Publishing
P.O. Box 143011
Irving, Texas 75014
Manufactured in the USA
10 9 8 7 6 5 4 3 2 1

Order of Collection

This Collection is dedicated to my wife Monica Hines and the Osby family

Best of the
Robert Hines Collection

An incomplete collection of works by the Deep Ellum Poet

I Heard

I heard the things you said my dear.
That's why I wish you could be near.
You know just how to make me smile,
I love you so, I'd walk for miles.
I heard you say you love me so,
Much more than I could every know.
Now have your feelings changed for me?

Tell me that this still could be.
I heard you say it would be nice,
Someday I hope you'll be my wife.
All these things they come in time.
One day all things will turn out fine.
I heard you when you were afraid.
You've got good reason to be that way.
I never meant to cause you hurt
All things you've said I've truly heard.

Robert Hines

To The Bone

I love you baby,
down to the bone.
If you'll be my lady,
I'll build you a throne.
I feel you
though we're far apart.
Your love goes much deeper
than Just in my heart.
There's reasons your love
has gotten to the bone.
You were so encouraging
when I stood alone.
The love that I have for you
has no measure,
You're truly worth more
than any lost treasure.
When you touch me
it goes straight to my bones,
Oh tell me that loving you
I can't go wrong.
I'm very amazed
that you care so for me.
It's with you
that I most certainly should be.
If you take me
you'll never be left all alone,
I pray that you miss me
this time that I'm gone.
Some day I will write you
the most beautiful love song,
My Love,
I love you
all the way To The Bone!

Robert Hines

All I Have

All I have is the memory
of our last conversation,
And it left me feeling
such a great sensation.
You said that you loved me
more than I'll every know,
I'm telling you lady,
that I need you so.
All I have is the memory
of holding you so tight,
It would be such a shame
without you in my life.
You've always made time for me
whenever it was needed,
Whenever I have knocked,
I've always been greeted.
All I have are the memories
of times you would scold me,
And the memory of just how mad
you would really be.
Sometimes through I'd wonder
if I had been fair.
All I have is the day
you said to me goodbye.
Are you willing to give
And have one really good try?
You know if I could
I would be right there.
So please don't give up,
'cause you're the only one that cared.

Robert Hines

The Moonlight

The moonlight shines oh so bright,
It comes around every night.
I've never known any other
To bring such happiness to many lovers,
The moonlight is so very blue,
Each night it shines so bright
for me and for you.
It's made my heart feel so many things,
For this is truly what the moonlight brings.
The moonlight shines for you and I,
Oh please say you'll give our love a try.
We've known each other for several years,
I really care for you,
so have no fear.
The moonlight gives lovers so much hope,
It's certainly from which such days
things are wrote.
Just to be with you
feels so right,
Come share with me tonight's moonlight.

Robert Hines

It Just Feels Good

It just feels good to know
that things will be okay.
For I truly trust the Lord
Not what people will say.
He's give me the words
To put into this poem,
When I die I'll go to heaven,
cause that's where I belong.
It just feels good to know,
That I've at least got one friend.
This friend has been around
And knows where I have been.
She's always been so sweet,
and thoughtful most times.
That's why she's now so blessed
She's truly very kind.
It just feels good to know,
That God looks out for me,
Cause if it weren't for Him,
I don't know where I'd be.
He's there when I am up,
And also when I'm down,
Everywhere that I have been,
He's surely been around.
It just feels so good,
To know you and the Lord,
I know the two of you,
won't let life be to hard.
The reason I know this,
You do what no one else would.
That's why knowing the two of you,
just really feels so good.

Robert Hines

I've Never Known

I've never known
a woman like you,
You've made my life
feel so brand new.
When I was down,
you were there
to show me just
how much you care.
I've never known
anyone so sweet,
You make my days
seem quite complete.
The things you say
make such good sense,
I hope that I'll
see you again.
I've never known
a lady so tender.
It's true.
You I'll always
remember.
When all my friends
had turned their back,
The things you said
were very exact.
I've never known
one as true,
You helped me
in hard times
to get through.
It seems all my life
I've been alone.
If not for you, I'd never have known.

Robert Hines

You Give Me

You give me so much
I don't know where to start.
It's not the material things,
but what comes from your heart.
Life was just seemed so simple
until I met you.
Now I'm so happy
I don't know what to do.
I am so very happy
cause you give me so much.
It started with your smile
and then came your touch.
Each time we get together
you give me something new.
Right now I really hope
this times we will get through.
You give me so much
I pray that you're all right.
I hope I'm not too late,
cause now I see the light.
Today I even have
a relationship with the Lord.
The stronger it gets,
it will not be destroyed.
You give me so much.
That's why I love you so.
The longer we're apart
the more our love can grow.
This time that we're apart
I feel it's in God's plan.
For he's preparing me
for a love that will withstand.

Robert Hines

Embrace the Joy

Embrace the things you feel
whenever I'm around.
For you are truly someone
that I am glad I found.
We aren't getting younger.
We're not little girls and boys.
Our time is very precious.
So let's embrace the joy.
You're often in my thoughts,
and of how I can please you.
I know one of the ways
is to stop some of the things I do.
Embrace the joy each day
in every way you can.
I feel the way we met
was the way that God had planned.
I always get the feeling
that I am special to you.
Please tell me what I'm thinking
is certainly the truth.
So talk the joy and love
that I've given you so far.
I've done all that I could,
at the time I had a car.
Embrace the joy and fun
that is yet to come.
Your life I will make happy.
I'll fill your days with fun.
If we fill our days with happiness
they'll outweigh our times apart.
So think of brighter days,
and embrace them all with joy.

Robert Hines

I Think I Feel You

I think I feel you
at this very minute.
I pray that you're happy.
No matter the ending.
Right now I know I hurt.
Now how about you?
Let me tell you something,
there's lots yet to be proved.
I think I feel you
cause right now I'm so mad,
Why didn't you say before,
the love for me you had.
It don't really matter
what I have to say,
You'll think like you want to,
cause you're set in your ways.
I think I feel you.
You said you loved me
that I know.
But let me tell you this:
I love you even more.
Sitting in my bed
at 3:00 AM this morning,
I missed you so much.
I was truly so lonely.
I think I feel you.
So say you'll give me a chance.
I'm filled with so much love,
and lots of romance.
It is not what I say,
but what I'm gonna do.
Cause when I get out, I need to feel you.

Robert Hines

I Rest My Case

You know I really Love you,
Of that there should be no doubt.
Just a few more things
that we need to straighten out.
You're very beautiful,
and certainly quite amazing.
I'm yours when you get ready
So now I rest my case.
There's nothing on this earth
That I won't do for you,
Though times right now are hard,
This mess we will get through.
Don't settle for being second,
You're first at any rate,
And soon there'll be no doubt.
Again I rest my case.
You said you'd be there for me,
But you needed a little space,
Take all the space you need,
Love never comes too late.
The way that we first started,
I know was sort of crazy,

But you know I Truly Love You.
That's it.
I rest my case.

Robert Hines

Sweet Sensation

Every since I've known you,
I truly have felt good,
You remind me of the things,
I used to read in books.
I've dreamed of meeting someone,
That has a lot of patience,
That's the reason that I think
You're such a sweet Sensation.
I remember those times
that we would ride around
searching for the things,
And a plenty we have found.
If I could have my way,
we'd travel the whole nation,
You're certainly more worthy,
you're my sweet sensation.
Don't you worry about nothing
cause the Lord is on our side,
He'll help us understand,
He'll help us do what's right.
You make my mind go black.
My heart begins to racing.
You mean the world to me.
You're such a
Sweet Sensation!!!

Robert Hines

Thanks

Thanks for being there when others turned away,
Thanks for helping me see I much be careful of what I pray.
Thanks for all the time that you've just listened to me,
Thanks for really being such a true friend indeed.
Thanks for the occasions that you've helped me smile,
Thanks for not leaving when I acted like a child.
Thanks for letting me know that I am very special to you,
Thanks for all the things that you've helped me to get through.
Thanks for telling me that you love me more than I know,
Thanks for letting me know that you truly need me so.
Thanks for being there when I had no where to turn,
Thanks for saying to me that your love someday I'll earn.
Thanks for the days that you'd take time out to be right there,
Thanks for all the moments you've made me feel you care.
Thanks most of all for showing your real concern,
Thanks to you so much, your love I truly yearn.

Robert L. Hines

When I See You

When I see you,
I get so much joy,
I'm reminded of the days
when I was a little boy.
My heart flutters
and my mind goes into rage,
You really do take me
to a whole new place.
When I see you,
it warms me all inside,
There's no place I'd rather be,
than right there by your side.
You look so sweet,
you're so unique,
Ever since I met you,
I now feel so complete.
When I see you,
I feel I'm on a cloud,
There'll be a day when I can say,
you've made me very proud.
It's just so many different things
that you make me feel,
I've never known another woman
that's ever been so real.
When I see you, the things you do,
makes my heart skip beats,
To me you're much more wonderful,
that the finest treats.
There's more I have to say,
so much I'm gonna do.
I pray, that you can wait,
till I can again see you.

Robert Hines

The Way I See It

Things will get better,
the way I see it.
Things just happen,
but don't you give up,
For the Lord is not going to
burden us with too much.
There just might be times
you won't feel a bit,
It will come to pass as I see it.
I have been wrong
a lot of different times,
Especially when I've told myself
everything was fine.
A lot of things in life
are still to come yet,
Just keep on living,
the way I see it.
When all the things in life
seem to go your way,
You feel that you should leave,
but instead just kneel and pray.
Don't do it to yourself,
don't take another hit,
Cause this too shall pass,
the way that I've seen it.
The more you love yourself,
the better you will feel,
Don't you give up on life,
cause everything's not real.

Robert Hines

The Last Tear Drop

It's all over now,
I'll cry no more,
This was the one
I so adored.
One day I awoke
and realized,
It's over now,
so say goodbye,
Enough with having
a broken heart,
This is indeed
the last tear drop.
I won't look back
cause there is so much pain,
For I did some things
that brought such shame.
We really tried
to make it through,
There was too much
we had to do.
It's all over now,
I've finally stopped,
This one's to you,
my last tear drop.

Robert Hines

My Love Will Never Die

All my life I've loved,
and I'll still continue to do so,
And often I've been through hurt sometimes,
I'll never give up though.
I've seen so many things,
and heard so many lies,
I promise this to you,
my love will never die.
There've been a few women,
that came along before you,
But what I like about you the most is,
you help me see the truth.
I'm not one to give up,
I'll give it my best
and certainly give us a try,
And if I don't and it doesn't work out,
don't mean my love will die.
Experience the day,
you let me in your life,
I wanted deep inside,
for you to be my wife.
This may seem strange to you,
but I've nothing to hide,
I have a love for you,
that will surely never die.
I've been so many places,
I've traveled lots of the world,
There's always been this search,
to just find the right girl.
It's been a lot of hurt
because I keep on trying,
One thing is for sure,
my love will never die.

Robert Hines

I Pledge

I pledge to make you happy
and give you all my love,
Cause one thing is for sure,
heaven's missing an angel above.
You make my life so happy,
and all my dreams come true,
You brighten all my days,
and make my gray skies blue.
I pledge to be your friend,
in desperate times of need,
There's nothing that I'll do,
unless we both agree.
On days you're feeling tired,
I make sure you can rest,
I'll give you what you need,
I'll always do my best.
I pledge to take you places,
that you have always dreamed,
It's hard to understand,
how others could treat you mean.
There's moments that you change,
but most times you're full of fun,
I think that we both know,
it's at my side you belong.
I pledge to give my heart,
in such a special way,
This is what I'll do for you
with each passing day.

Robert Hines

Even When

I loved you even when they said you were no good,
Cause you were right there when no one else understood.
However hard it was you didn't give up and leave,
I wish that you really wanted to be with me indeed.
You were listening even when things I said didn't make any sense,
Believe me when I say, that it's you I truly miss.
I feel even though I know that you're not here,
When I go to sleep at night in my dreams you appear.
I cared for you even when you said that you weren't ready,
My emotions for you run very hard and really steady.
It's not ever a problem if there'll be days you're sort of sick,
Fit it's you my precious that I so long to be with.
I'll want you even when times are going to be hard,
There'll never be nothing that can pull our love apart.
See in my eyes you're the lady that I chose to be with.
That's why no matter what happens, I love you even then.

Robert Hines

Let's Make Love

Let me take you home after a good time,
I know you would like to be wined and dined.
When I get you home, please take off your shoes,
There's lots of things left that we're going to do.
This will be a night that's sent from above,
Come here my sweet, it's time to make love.
Let's light a few candles and turn off the lights,
Just lay back and enjoy what I do tonight.
We'll take a warm bath and I'll rub you in oil,
It's you so indeed, that I'm going to spoil.
You'll feel like you're flying, just like a great dove,
Come with me tonight. It's time we make love.
I've watched you so long over the years,
Now I'm finding out that you are so dear.
Who would have thought you'd be with this stud.
So come here sweet lady, it's time to make love.

Robert Hines

Thinking about You

When I think of you,
it just drives me wild.
You've got such a great body,
I love it when you smile.
It took me some time
to build up my nerves.
Let me give you the lovin'
that you so deserve.
Whether you know it or not,
you make gray skies blue,
It just comes so easy
when I write about you.
When I think about you,
my mind goes down so far,
You've truly got a figure,
that's fit to be a star.
This may to you seem far fetched,
it may seem very strange,
What I'm gonna do to you
might make you wanna change.
I'm going to make you Platinum,
I will fulfill your wish.
When I think of you,
my heart just skips a beat,
So open up real wide,
and let me kiss those cheeks.
I want to get to know you,
and everything you do,
Cause so much comes to mind,
when I'm thinking about you!!!

Robert Hines

You're Tops

I've known a few women
in my time of life,
There was even one
I though would be my wife.
In spite of everything,
I cared for her a lot.
But you compared to her,
I tell you that you're tops.
I won't bore you with comparisons,
cause with you there are none.
The moments we have shared
have been filled with so much fun.
You make me feel so good,
I think that you're so hot,
I tell once again,
I think you're really tops.
If I could rule the world,
I'd choose you as my Queen,
No matter what you'd want,
I'd give you anything.
A lot of things I've done
have put me on the spot,
Now there's no doubt to me,
I know you're truly tops.
You know I surely love you,
cause I keep coming back,
There's nothing on this earth
that I can tell you lack.
The things I use to do,
I know I have to stop,
I know it will be worth it,
cause I know that you are tops.

Robert Hines

Could It Be

Could it be,
I've found my dreams,
Cause with you
my life has meaning.
I've had times
my life was so sad,
You changed my hurt,
you made me glad.
Could it be,
you are for me?
I cannot change
the things I see.
My life's been full
of ups and downs,
All that has changed
since you I've found.
Could it be
that I'm your knight.
I'll do the things,
to make it right.
There's no one else
that I care for.
You know it's you
I so adore.
Could it be
you love me too,
There's lots of things
we both can do.
Of all the things
that I have seen,
Could it be
this ain't a dream.

Robert Hines

Don't Get Confused

Don't confuse the meaning
of a true friend indeed,
Cause friends don't have to beg
for things they really need.
Sometimes I get mixed up,
the things inside my head,
I've done a lot of things
that I truly dread.
Don't get confused my friend,
the color of my skin,
Just because I'm Black
doesn't mean I'm filled with sin,
I've heard it said before,
that we all look alike,
Everything that you hear
ain't necessarily right.
Don't get confused.
The anger that shows
outside of me,
It's just a great big mask
for all the world to see.
At times I get so mad,
I don't know what to do,
That's when the Lord Jesus,
seems to get me through.
Don't confuse my kindness,
as a sign of being weak,
Cause I can become something
you really don't want to see.
You need to know
that I don't like being used.
I'll be your friend indeed,
but don't get me confused.

Robert Hines

Wishing You Were Near

I'm sitting here alone you think,
but I know better,
Cause my mind is on you.
I'm not thinking about the weather.
This may seem very bad,
yet it's not as things appear.
No matter what you feel,
I'm wishing you were near.
If I just had one picture
it would fill my soul.
For you mean more to me
than any amount of gold.
Our friendship that we share
has come upon a year,
And I have got no doubt
that we have gotten nearer.
I know my past looks bad,
but all my life you've changed.
The thing you do for me
just makes me feel so sane.
Now don't you have no doubt,
don't you have no fears,
Cause all I'm doing now
is wishing you were near.
As I look back over the days,
you too had your fits.
And I know this is just something
I'll have to put up with.
I pray that all our days
will turn into lots of years,
No matter, however long.
I'll be wishing you were near.

Robert Hines

I'm Looking

I'm looking for a lady
that's willing to take the time
To correspond with me
just a very few lines.
I don't know what to say.
I'm just a nice Black man.
That got caught in a situation
that surely wasn't planned.
I'm looking for a woman
who wants a man like me.
Cause I am really simple,
though in love I've got degrees.
Oh yes, I specialize in love
that comes straight from the heart.
That's why if you write me,
my love will not depart.
I'm looking for someone
that will be there for me.
Whenever times get hard,
I won't just up and leave.
You might think this is all
that I'd have to say.
If you accept my offer,
so much will come your way.
I'm looking for that lady
that wants to be a Queen.
For when I'm in the world,
you'll have most everything.
Don't worry 'bout a thing.
Cause I will share the cooking.
So tell me you're the one,
of which I have been looking.

Robert Hines

When I Fall In Love

When I fall in love
I give it my all.
For I try to think you're the one.
Each day I try to call.
At times we won't agree
on each and everything.
But that's what makes love grow.
It gives our lives some meaning.
When I fall in love,
I try to look inside.
Cause I don't want to run.
No I don't want to hide.
I know when you're in love
it's not about the beauty.
It should be on how well
each one can do their duties.
When I fall in love
I'll try to keep you happy.
I know there will be times
that you will be demanding.
That's when I do my best
to try to keep you pleased.
Since you came in my life
you have fulfilled my needs.
When I fall in love,
it's because you really care.
I'll try to do the same.
I'll truly be as fair.
I know there will be times
on things we won't agree.
Because when I'm in love,
it's cause you don't love me.

Robert Hines

My Love for You

Although our love is far apart,
You still remain within my heart.

There may even be another man,
But you must know that I understand.

The things I feel seem so unreal,
Cause you give me so much reason to Live.

My love for you is so very strong,
I count the minutes as I stand alone.

You picked me up when I was down,
I thank you for this love I've found.

Each day goes by you're on my mind,
That's why I think of you all the time.

I hope these words you also feel,
For I miss you so, though we're not near.

Just knowing this thought can someday be true,
I'll keep on saving my love for you!

Robert Hines

I Await

I await the day that I'll find true love,
For my heart just can't hold a grudge.

My heart and mind will always forgive,
See I've learned this through this life I've lived.

The riches of this world I may never acquire,
Yet my heart is filled with so much desire.

I await the time that our eyes will meet,
And you'll invite me over to have a seat.

From that day forward our love will grow,
It will be a moment that we'll both know.

Our days and nights
will feel like fantasies and dreams,
The love is fit like clothes so well seamed.

I await the day that you come into my life,
My promise is that I'll make things turn out right.

What we have will contain the main ingredient,
Cause our main love will be the love of Jesus.

That day in life will surely come to pass,
And when it does I'll do my best to make it last.

Robert Hines

The Gift Of Love

I've finally discovered the gift of love,
It came through earth's angels but it was sent from above.

Just to realize that I'd loved all the wrong things,
For my love was for money, women, and all life's games.

Today I have a splendid gift of love,
And now my life isn't so empty or dull.

There's no need to sit around and feel all bad,
Cause you see this kind of life just makes us sad.

The gift of love can set you free,
It's right there for you or me.

Each day is but a new reprieve,
So go to Jesus with your needs.

The gift of love comes from the skies,
Yes it will give you a brand new high.

Remember each day to say your prayers,
And know and believe Lord Jesus will always be there.

Robert Hines

Accused

I've been accused of lots of things,
And it really hurts when you're trying to change.

Now make no mistake I've done lots of harm,
But I never ever meant to do others wrong.

I've been accused when things come up missing,
There was a time that I know I've been guilty.

Today this is something I don't worry about,
Yet all around there's still much doubt.

I've been accused no matter where I go,
Oh don't they know that I love them so,

Day by day grows a change in me,
Inside me is still a growing disease.

I've been accused of being a nothing,
Inside of my heart I just keep on searching.

What I know is I only have this day,
Just thank you Lord Jesus is all I can say.

Robert Hines

I'll Cherish

I'll cherish the moments that we spend together,
Through winter, spring, summer, and fall weather.

Our evenings will be filled with so much romance,
And we'll make love each time there's a chance.

I'll cherish our days and always love you,
There's just so many things that we can do.

You'll never really guess how much you mean to me,
But each day that passes you will begin to see.

I'll cherish each time when you pick up the phone,
For I truly do miss you at times I'm all alone.

If you can relate to the way that I feel,
Then we're well on our way to a love that is real.

Robert Hines

More than Just Words

The things I write are more than just words,
Instead they're what I lived and not what I heard.

My life has been as many have dared to dream,
And been proportionate to both life's extremes.

Everyone wants to live life on its most high,
But when it's not that way you often wonder why.

Yes, these things I write are more than words,
They're the roads I traveled and its many curves.

Until I found the Lord who's really my best friend,
I thought the rough road would never, ever end.

Now I know my life's more than what's been said,
Cause what I write about is more than just words.

Robert Hines

Lives

Inside each of us there are two sides,
But what we don't realize is our many lives.

There's one for work and there's one for play,
Part of us wants to go and the other wants to stay.

Most don't see the many changes in ourselves,
Soon we're so mixed up until there's little left.

The biggest part of us survive on common sense,
And the rest of us are mixed up about the way life is meant.

These lives can go to so many different extremes,
Most people are nice and others are quite mean.

Everybody gets mixed up at one point or another,

Our lives have been built through our experiences in life,
I can only hope that soon we'll give Jesus a try.

Robert Hines

Our Children

I ask you America
How can we take better care of our children
when these prices of things aren't ever descending,

I ask you America
Isn't it really hard to give our kids more time
when we have to work two jobs just to survive.

I ask you America
Do you think that buying these things replaces love
cause it only makes our children only seek blood.

I ask you America
From where are all these fatal messages sent,
for most of us want to blame our government.

I say to you America
Give our children more teachings of the Lord,
just use your life experiences and it really won't be that hard.

Robert Hines

What Happened

What happened to the caring world,
now so caught up in world affairs.
It just seems that it's all about worldly things,
and we're losing concern for our human beings.

What happened to all the loving hearts,
it appears that our families are pulling apart.
Blaming each other when things go wrong,
sometimes ending up in bodily harm.

What happened to the followers of Jesus,
for they claim that they are true believers.
It just seems that this world is so unfair,
cause there's just so few that's left to care.

What happened to those that trust,
when it comes to the Lord this is a must.
All of the world is just so much afraid,
so remember that each of us the Father made.

Robert Hines

Poets

I sit in a room of minds, each with a great idea.
Ideas are rambling and pens are reaching papers with thought.
What a great gift we have and so many will miss the miracle,
due to the fears of really getting to know themselves.
As for me I know I'm a lot of great things and
a great many bad things also.

Some look at me and say there's another crack head
but they could be right and wrong at the same time.
As I write I hurt so inside and I'm trying to find a way
to communicate with those who are so dear to me.

Mankind, now you think you know how easy it is but do
you know how many times I really truly tried.
I know you can relate to being betrayed
but does anyone in this room know
how many times it's happened to me.

Stop looking at me on the outside because there
you'll find only what seems to be true.
Instead let's have a cup of coffee sometime
and share our feelings with one another.
For it is only there that we will

Robert Hines

Shelf

I put all my characteristics on a shelf,
And for awhile it seemed there was nothing else.

Everything about me required a change,
It was either that or I'd go insane

All of my characteristics that were put on a shelf,
Are still there waiting just to be felt.

You see there are things that come up in life,
My old feelings jump up and I often wonder why.

I must remember that all that I had,
Is right there on a shelf including my getting mad.

There's just one thing that's not on my shelf.
That's my teachings of Jesus cause he's all that I have left.

Robert Hines

Pride

This thing called pride has two sides,
There's one with understanding and another you'll hide.

One thing that I know is that pride can be false,
It can hide what you're feeling so much 'til you're lost.

If you take it to your head you might end up dead,
Or at least you'll end up feeling you're dead.

Pride and ego are very much kin,
Cause each of the two are really of form of sin.

Who really cares if you're right or you know,
For the only thing it gives is standing a fall or afloat.

Just remember that pride can be put to the side,
And it's replaced with humbling to smooth out the stride.

Robert Hines

Thanks Oprah

A while back I wrote this poem,
And it was just for you.
But what I saw today,
I should have done this sooner.
Each show that you do,
You do it with your heart.
I see you fighting tears
That really was so hard.
Now what I'm talking 'bout
Was your interview with Luther?
You did it with such grace
You've never been a user.
You didn't just stop with him,
You also showed his Mother.
The tears you made me cry,
I felt I was his Brother.
Dig so deep inside.
The work you do is thorough.
You dig so deep inside.
You help them look within.
You help them swallow pride.
I've seen you have your battles
With different things in life,
But most of all I've noticed,
You want to do what's right.
This poem does not repeat
It's title over and over,
Cause there's so much I've missed,
I wish I could say more.
But just so you will know,
This poem's just for you.
I'd like to thank you Oprah.
You helped me see the truth.

Robert Hines

You're truly a Great Man

As I sit and listen
To your miracle re-teachings,
I realized just how much
of my life had no meaning.
You gave me the encouragement
To write once again;
Mr. Luther Vandross,
You're truly a great man.
I realize how much of life
I've taken for granted.
There's been so many times
I've failed whenever demanded.
Most things I've tried to do
Didn't go as planned,
My hat's off to you.
For you're truly great men.
I'm so amazed
When I see how hard you try.
It surely can be no doubt
The Lord is on your side.
So many take for granted
Just the fact that they can stand,
Although to you it's now hard too,
You're truly a great man.
If I could give you anything
To show how much I care,
Right now I'd take your place.
That just seems so fair.
You've said things in your song
to help me in romance.
My thanks I give you Luther,
You're truly a great man.

Robert Hines

The Poet Robert L. Hines, a Marine Corp veteran, was born in deep East Texas on a dairy farm in the small town of Carthage. He was raised by his parents, Sefron and Cassie Hines. Robert attended Carthage public schools through the 11th grade. During this time, he learned carpentry and auto mechanics well enough to support an independent life style. At an early age he was introduced to drugs and alcohol, which eventually led him into a drug rehabilitation center. In November 1995, while in rehab, he began to write poetry. The writing was much needed therapy to sobriety he so desperately sought. He wrote day and night. The more he wrote, the more he felt he had to write. A friend who was also in drug recovery, asked Robert if he could take a copy of his poems home with him upon the completion of his rehab program. He told Robert that the poems were good and that he really enjoyed them. Robert allowed him to take the work. He took the work home where he typed and organized it. When he returned the work he said to Robert, "Now go and make a living with your Poetry." He encouraged Robert to continue to write poems, because he felt that people would love the work. That's what Robert did and continues to do. He became artist–in-residence in **Deep Ellum downtown Dallas**, where he is known as the Deep Ellum Poet. For ten years Robert wrote poems on many different subjects that were influenced by his life struggles and experiences. He states, "I hope that in reading my poetry, one will find something that strikes a chord within themselves that will cause one to say, yes, I feel that way; or yes, I've felt that feeling; or most importantly; yes, maybe GOD can also help me to change, for GOD is so good, look what he's done for Robert.

\\

Notes

Deep Ellum Facts

https://en.wikipedia.org/wiki/Deep_Ellum,_Dallas

Deep Ellum's claim to fame has been its music. By the 1920s, the neighborhood had become a hotbed for early jazz and blues musicians, hosting the likes of Blind Lemon Jefferson, Robert Johnson, Huddie "Lead Belly" Ledbetter, and Bessie Smith in Deep Ellum clubs like The Harlem and The Palace.[17] From 1920 to 1950, the number of nightclubs, cafes and domino parlors in Deep Ellum jumped from 12 to 20.

In 1937, a columnist described Deep Ellum as:

...[the] one spot in the city that needs no daylight saving time because there is no bedtime...[It is] the only place recorded on earth where business, religion, hoodooism, gambling and stealing goes on at the same time without friction...Last Saturday a prophet held the best audience in this 'Madison Square Garden' in announcing that Jesus Christ would come to Dallas in person in 1939. At the same time a pickpocket was lifting a week's wages from another guy's pocket, who stood with open mouth to hear the prophecy.

At the time, you could find gun and locksmith shops, clothing stores, the Cotton Club, tattoo studios, barber-shops, pawn shops, drugstores, tea rooms, loan offices, domino halls, pool halls, and walk-up hotels. On its sidewalks you could find pigeon droppers, reefer men, craps shooters, card sharps, and sellers of cocaine and marijuana.[18] Sometime around World War I, Lead Belly and Blind Lemon Jefferson got together and began composing folk tunes, with Dallas often in the lyrics. In a song called "Take A Whiff on Me":

Walked up Ellum an' I come down Main,
Tryin' to bum a nickel jes' to buy cocaine.
Ho, Ho, baby, take a whiff on me.[18]

The most famous song about the district was recorded in 1933 under the title of "Deep Elm Blues" by the Lone Star Cowboys. The song and the lyrics were derived from the Georgia Crackers' 1927 recording, "The Georgia Black Bottom." The Shelton Brothers recorded "Deep Elem Blues" on Decca in 1935. Despite these earlier recordings, they claimed credit for the song. The lyrics narrate white men seeking immoral and illegal entertainment in an African American part of town. The Shelton Brothers iterated the name of the district in "Deep Elem Blues, No. 2," "What's the Matter with Deep Elem," and "Deep Elm Boogie Woogie Blues." Dick Stabile and his Orchestra, the Texas Wanderers, and the Wilburn Brothers all invoked the district's name in separate Decca pressings.

"Deep Ellum Blues" was later performed by the Grateful Dead:

When you go down on Deep Ellum,
Put your money in your socks
'Cause them Women on Deep Ellum
Sho' will throw you on the rocks. (chorus)
Oh, sweet mama, your daddy's got them Deep Ellum Blues.
Oh, sweet mama, your daddy's got them Deep Ellum Blues.

Bob Dylan's new album "Rough And Rowdy Ways" (release June 19, 2020) has the song "Murder Most Foul" with the line "... / When you're down on Deep Ellum, put your money in your shoe /..." (© & P Columbia Records)

Following World War II, the success of Deep Ellum started to fade. The ever-growing availability and use of the automobile led to the removal of the Houston and Texas Central railroad tracks—to make way for Central Expressway—and by 1956 the streetcar line had been removed. Businesses closed, residents moved to the suburbs and the music all but stopped. In 1969, a new elevation of Central Expressway truncated Deep Ellum, completely obliterating the 2400 block of Elm Street, viewed by many as the center of the neighborhood. By the 1970s, few original businesses remained and its homeless population began to grow.

Other Work by Robert Hines
Selected Works by Robert L. Hines "The Deep Ellum Poet"
The Inspired Works by Robert L. Hines "The Deep Ellum Poet"

Cheudi Publishing

Since 2003
P.O. Box 143011
Irving, Texas 75014

www.ingramcontent.com/pod-product-compliance
Lightning Source LLC
Chambersburg PA
CBHW080817250626
47159CB00010B/3423